D0919958

AN ABBEY THEATRE COMMISSION

FIRE BELOW (A WAR OF WORDS)

OWEN MCCAFFERTY

A co-production between the
Abbey Theatre and the Lyric Theatre

Lyric Theatre

The Lyric Theatre in Belfast makes a unique and vital contribution to the community as the only full-time producing theatre in Northern Ireland.

Employing local actors, including Liam Neeson, Ciarán Hinds and Adrian Dunbar at early stages of their careers, its mission is to produce high-quality professional theatre that is alive to the complex cultural experience and diverse traditions of Northern Ireland, and to use the power of live theatre to inspire, engage, educate and empower.

From first rehearsal to final curtain, the shows we create are truly indigenous products of Northern Ireland. Putting local issues and local characters centre stage is what the Lyric does best. Our shows are relevant to local audiences and revealing to visitors to the city. And a very important part of the Lyric Theatre's strategy is to tour as widely as possible, to give audiences outside Northern Ireland an insight into our culture and to the work of the Lyric.

Officially opened in May 2011 by Brian Friel, the Lyric's new home on the banks of Belfast's River Lagan, on the site of the previous theatre, is a landmark £18.1m building that signals the continued regeneration of the city and is a catalyst for real progress in arts infrastructure for artists and audiences alike.

Designed by O'Donnell + Tuomey, and built in a stunning blend of Belfast brick, glass, steel, concrete and Iroko timber, the new theatre is alive and dramatic at all times. Spacious lobbies and bars overlooking the river, and two beautiful auditoria with an exciting artistic programme, makes the Lyric a thriving social hub, creative learning space and a real attraction for visitors to the city.

PRINCIPAL FUNDER

MAIN STAGE SPONSOR

ALSO FUNDED BY

CORPORATE LOUNGE SPONSOR

AbbeyBondLovis

THE LYRIC IS ALSO GENEROUSLY SUPPORTED BY

IN-KIND SPONSORS

DIRECT WINE SHIPMENTS

LYRIC THEATRE STAFF

ABBEY
THEATRE
AMHARCLANN
NA MAINISTREACH

INSPIRED BY THE revolutionary ideals of its
founders and its rich canon of Irish dramatic
writing, the Abbey Theatre's mission is
to imaginatively engage with all of Irish
society through the production of ambitious,
courageous and new theatre in all its forms.
The Abbey Theatre commits to lead in the
telling of the whole Irish story, in English
and in Irish, and affirms that it is a theatre
for the entire island of Ireland and for all its
people. In every endeavour, the Abbey Theatre
promotes inclusiveness, diversity and equality.

ABBEY THEATRE SUPPORTERS

FUNDERS AND PARTNERS

ARCHIVE PARTNER OF THE ABBEY THEATRE

An Roinn
Cultúir, Oidhreachta agus Gaeltachta

Department of
Culture, Heritage and the Gaeltacht

 Irish Life

RTÉ
SUPPORTING THE
arts

CORPORATE GUARDIANS

 THE DOYLE COLLECTION

The Westbury Hotel
DUBLIN

THE DOYLE COLLECTION, OFFICIAL HOTEL PARTNER OF IRELAND'S NATIONAL THEATRE.

Irish Life

BROWN THOMAS   McCANN FITZGERALD
ESTABLISHED 1849 ADORED EVER SINCE

ARTHUR COX   Bank of Ireland

ABBEY THEATRE SUPPORTERS

PROGRAMME SUPPORT
Bank of America Merrill
Lynch
The O'Neill Family
The Cielinski Family
Diageo Ireland
Friends First
RTÉ Supporting the Arts
Vintners' Federation of
Ireland
Avantcard
The Ireland Fund of Great
Britain

GOLD AMBASSADORS
Credit Suisse

SILVER AMBASSADORS
101 Talbot Restaurant
Clarion Consulting Limited
Conway Communications
DCC plc
FCm Travel Solutions
Irish Poster Advertising
Manor House Hotels
of Ireland
National Radio Cabs
Paddy Power
RSM
Sims IVF
Sisk Steconfer Joint
Venture
Utilities Ltd
John Sisk and Son
Spector Information
Security
The Church Bar &
Restaurant
The Merrion Hotel
Trocadero
Webfactory
Wynn's Hotel
Zero-G

DIRECTORS' CIRCLE
Tony Ahearne
Bill Baroni
Richard and Sherril
Burrows
Pat Butler
The Cielinski Family
John Connors
Dónall Curtin
Mark and Tobey Dichter
Roma Downey
Deirdre Finan
Janice Flynn
Honorable Elizabeth
Frawley Bagley
Emer and Basil Geoghegan
James Healy
Marjorie and Simon
Hewett
Declan Kelly
Bernard and Muriel
Lauren Foundation
Paul Lonergan
John Leahy
Dwayne and Eimear
Lysaght
Robert and Cynthia
McCann
Mick and Claire
McCormack
James McNally
Peter Merrigan
Donal Moore
Larry Moulter and
Pamela Frechette
William O'Connor
Sheelagh O'Neill
Thomas F and Carol
O'Neill
Tom and Shelly O'Neill
Sarah and Sean Reynolds
Mark Ryan
Mike Sheehan

Michael Walsh and
Therese Quinn
Steve and Mitra Van
Mark Walsh
Zachary Webb
Lloyd Weinreb

SILVER PATRONS
James Adrian
Majella Altschuler
Robert D Bickford Jr
Frances Britton
Catherine Byrne
Tommy Gibbons
James Hickey
Liam and Eibhlin Howard
Bogdan and
Holly Kaczmarczyk
Dr. John Keane
Andrew Mackey
Eugenie Mackey
Eugene Magee
John and Irene McGrane
Gerard and Liv
McNaughton
Pat Moylan
Alan O'Sullivan
Marie Rogan and
Paul Moore
Judge Felice R. Stack
Jan Velund
Eileen Shields-West

Fire Below (A War of Words), a co-production between the Abbey Theatre, Dublin, and the Lyric Theatre, Belfast, was first performed on the Danske Bank stage of the Lyric Theatre, Belfast, on 12 October 2017 and on the Peacock stage of the Abbey Theatre, Dublin, on 7 November 2017. The cast was as follows:

cast (in order of appearance)

Rosemary	Cara Kelly
Gerry	Frankie McCafferty
Tom	Ruairi Conaghan
Maggie	Ali White

production credits

Director	Jimmy Fay
Assistant Director	Emily Foran
Set Design	Paula McCafferty
Costume Design	Úna Hickey
Costume Supervisor	Gillian Lennox
Costume Assistant	Erin Charteris
Music and Sound Design	Conor Mitchell
Lighting Design	Sinead McKenna
AV Consultant	Neil O'Driscoll
Production Managers	Paul Hinchcliffe
	Cliff Barragry
Casting Directors	Kelly Phelan
	Clare Gault
Company Stage Managers	Anne Kyle
	Kate Miller
Deputy Stage Manager	Aimee Yates
Assistant Stage Manager	Stephen Dix
Technical Manager	Keith Ginty
Technicians	Damian Cox
	Ian Vennard
Apprentice Technician	Conal Clapper
Set Builders	Noel Woods
	Mark McPhilips

Thanks to Harriet Fay, Tom Gallagher & Aine Ni Fiaich

Biographies

OWEN MCCAFFERTY

WRITER

OVER THE PAST TWENTY-FIVE YEARS OWEN MCCAFFERTY'S PLAYS HAVE BEEN PERFORMED worldwide and have won numerous awards. Previous work includes *Titanic: Scenes from the British Wreck Commissioner's Inquiry, 1912* (MAC, Belfast); *The Absence of Women* (Lyric Theatre, Belfast, and Tricycle Theatre, London); *Days of Wine and Roses* (Donmar Theatre, London; *Closing Time* (National Theatre, London); *Shoot the Crow* (Druid, Galway); *Mojo Mickybo* (Kabosh, Belfast); *Scenes from the Big Picture* (National Theatre, London), which won the Meyer-Whitworth, John Whiting and Evening Standard Awards; *Quietly* (Abbey Theatre, Dublin), which won the Writer's Guild Award for Best Play; and *Death of a Comedian* (Abbey Theatre, Dublin, Lyric Theatre, Belfast, and Soho Theatre, London). He is currently working on his first screenplay, *Normal People* and a musical based on the novel *The Good Son*.

CARA KELLY
ROSEMARY

CARA PREVIOUSLY PLAYED Maggie in *Dancing at Lughnasa* at the Lyric in 2015. She also worked with playwright Owen McCafferty in *Unfaithful* at the Traverse Theatre for the Edinburgh Festival. Her other theatre credits include: *Molly Maggie Mundy Sweeney* (Citizen Theatre) for which Cara won Best Actor from the Critics' Award for Theatre in Scotland; *On Raftery's Hill* (Druid Theatre Company), *Translations* (Donmar), *The Steward of Christendom* (Gate Dublin and Royal Court), *King Lear* and *All Things Nice* (Royal Court), *The Beauty Queen of Leenane, Romeo and Juliet, The Importance of Being Earnest*, and *Macbeth* (Royal Lyceum Edinburgh), *Unfaithful* (Traverse Edinburgh), *Elizabeth Gordon Quinn* (National Theatre of Scotland), *Henry VIII* (RSC), *Top Girls* (Old Vic, Stoke), *Life of Galileo* (Almeida), *Miss Julie* (Young Vic), *You Never Can Tell* (West Yorkshire Playhouse), *The Odd Couple* (female version, Perth Theatre). TV and film credits include: *Rillington Place* (BBC), *Sunday* (Channel 4), *The Precious Blood, Holy Cross* (BBC NI), *Taggart* (STV), *State of Play, Waterloo Rd, Trust Me* (BBC), *Shetland, Garrow's Law, River City, Monarch of the Glen, Rebus* (BBC1 Scotland). Cara is a previous winner of the Radio 4 Carleton Hobbs Award and was a member of the Radio Drama Company.

FRANKIE MCCAFFERTY
GERRY

FRANKIE MCCAFFERTY TRAINED AT THE Conservatoire National Superieur d'Art Dramatique, Paris. He most recently appeared in *The Weir* at the Lyric Theatre, Belfast in a co-production with Decadent Theatre. He has both directed and performed at the Lyric, where roles have included *Conversations on a Homecoming, Arms and the Man, The Shadow of a Gunman, Molly Sweeney, Much Ado About Nothing, The Crucible, Dealers Choice* (Prime Cut co-production) *Bah Humbug, Little Red Riding Hood* and *Observe the Sons of Ulster Marching towards the Somme* (Irish Times award Best Supporting Actor). At the Abbey Theatre he appeared in Tom Murphy's *The Patriot Game* and in *The Plough and the Stars* in 2010 and 2012. Other favourite roles have been in Mark Doherty's *Trad* (Galway Arts Festival) which won an Edinburgh Fringe First and Adelaide Fringe Awards, Samuel Beckett's *Endgame* (Prime Cut Productions) and *Ohio Impromptu* (Happy Days Festival, Enniskillen), Conal Creedon's *Second City Trilogy* at the Half Moon Theatre, Cork, Sam Thompson's *Over the Bridge* at the Waterfront Studio, and in Conor McPherson's *The Seafarer* (Decadent Theatre, Irish Times Best Supporting Actor Nomination). With Druid Theatre Company he appeared in John B Keane's *Sharon's Grave* (Irish Times Best Actor nomination), *At the Black Pig's Dyke* (Belfast Telegraph EMA award Best Actor), *Wild Harvest, The Song of the Yellow Bittern, Silverlands* and *Shadow and Substance*. Extensive TV credits include most recently *Vikings, Charlie, Twenty Twelve, Ripper Street* and *My Mother and other Strangers*, and a favourite role was in Ali White's *Any Time Now*. He appeared in all six seasons of *Ballykissangel*, as well as in films including *Philomena, Angela's Ashes, Fifty Dead Men Walking, In the Name of the Father* and *Fools of Fortune*. He can shortly be seen on screen in the upcoming *Rebellion 2* and *The Woman in White*.

RUAIRI CONAGHAN
TOM

RUAIRI'S THEATRE CREDITS INCLUDE: *Educating Rita* (Queens Theatre Hornchurch); *Easter Rising and Thereafter* (Jermyn St/West End); *Hamlet* (Barbican); *The Bombing of the Grand Hotel* (Cockpit London/Brighton Festival); *Theatre Uncut* (Soho Theatre); *Molly Sweeney* (London Print Room/ Lyric Theatre Belfast Tour); *All That Fall* (Arts Theatre West End/59e59 New York); *Philadelphia Here I Come* (Donmar Warehouse); *Truth and Reconciliation* and *Trust* (Royal Court); *Scenes From The Big Picture* and *Peer Gynt* (RNT); *The White Star of the North, The Crucible, Tearing The Loom, A Midsummer Nights Dream*, and *Put Out That Light* (Lyric Theatre Belfast); *Philadelphia Here I Come* (Wyndhams West End/US Tour, Lyric theatre Belfast); *Factory Girls*

(Arcola); *I Like Mine With a Kiss* (The Bush); *Kitty and Damnation* (Lion and Unicorn); *A Thousand Yards* (Southwark Playhouse); *Elegies* and *Green Orange and Pink* (Kings Head/West End); *Someone To Watch Over Me* (Theatre Royal Northampton); *Port Authority, The White Devil, Othello, School For Scandal*, and *Fall From Grace* (Liverpool Everyman); *Across The Barricades* (New Victoria Stoke); *Rough Justice, Box*, and *Ruffian On the Stair* (Northcott Theatre); *Blood Sweat and Tears* (Big Telly); *That Driving Ambition* (Replay). TV and Film: *Hamlet* (NT Live); *Downton Abbey* (Carnival/ ITV); *The Suspicions Of Mr Whicher* (Hat Trick/ ITV); *The Bill* and *Frances Tuesday* (ITV); *Doctors* and *Best: His Mothers Son, The Catherine Tate Show, Waking The Dead, Silent Witness, Murphy's Law*, and *Supergrass* (BBC); *An Officer From France* (RTE). Radio: *Juno and the Paycock, An Angel at My Table, The Lonely Passion Of Judith Hearne, The Man From God Knows Where* (BBC Radio). Sunday Times TMA Nomination: Best Supporting Actor, *Philadelphia Here I Come*.

ALI WHITE
MAGGIE

RECENT THEATRE WORK INCLUDES: *The Effect* (Rough Magic); *LIPPY* (DeadCentre); *Northern Star* (Rough Magic – ITTA 2016 Best Supporting Actress); *Bailed Out!* (Fishamble); *Deadly* (Abbey Theatre); *God of Carnage* (Prime Cut) and *Major Barbara* (Abbey Theatre).

Other work includes: *Romeo & Juliet, The House, Dancing at Lughnasa, Translations, Philadelphia Here I Come, The Trojan Women* (Abbey Theatre); *Catastrophe, Come and Go, Play, The Double Dealer, A Midsummer Night's Dream* (Gate Theatre); *Spokesong, School For Scandal, Lady Windermere's Fan, Love and A Bottle* (Rough Magic); *Playhouse Creatures* (The Old Vic); *The Importance of Being Earnest* (West Yorkshire Playhouse); *The Silver Tassie* (Almeida); *The Steward of Christendom* (Out of Joint); *Playboy of the Western World, Oliver Twist, The Importance of Being Earnest* and *All Souls' Night* (Lyric Theatre). Recent film & TV work includes: *The Bailout; Cellar Door; Acceptable Risks; The Fall; The Secret; The Truth Commissioner* and Simon Fitzmaurice's *My Name is Emily.* Writing work includes: *Me, Mollser* (Abbey Theatre Community & Education Department); *Catching the Fly* (BBC Radio 4)*; The Clinic* (Parallel Films/RTE); and *Any Time Now* (BBC/RTE).

JIMMY FAY
DIRECTOR

JIMMY IS THE EXECUTIVE PRODUCER OF the Lyric Theatre, Belfast, where he has directed productions of *The Ladykillers* by Graham Linehan, *St. Joan* by Bernard Shaw, *Here Comes the Night,* by Rosemary Jenkinson, *Pentecost,* by Stewart Parker, *Mixed Marriage* by St John Ervine and *True West* by Sam Shepard. He has been an Associate Artist of the Abbey Theatre,

having also spent time there as Staff Director, Associate Director and Literary Director. Directing work at the Abbey includes the acclaimed production of Owen McCafferty's *Quietly* (also toured to Edinburgh Festival Fringe 2013 and the Irish Rep, New York 2016), *The Risen People, The Government Inspector, Curse of the Starving Class, Macbeth, The Playboy of the Western World, Ages of the Moon, The Resistable Rise of Arturo Ui, The Seafarer, Saved, The School for Scandal, Howie the Rookie, True West, Henry IV, The Muesli Belt, At Swim-Two-Birds, Melonfarmer* and *The Papar.* In New York he directed the world premiere production of Sam Shepard's play *Ages of the Moon* starring Stephen Rea at the Atlantic Theatre. Jimmy was the first Director of the Dublin Fringe Festival and Artistic Director of Bedrock Productions. Directing credits there include the Irish premiers of *This Is Our Youth, Roberto Zucco, Blasted, Night Just Before The Forest, Quay West,* and *Faraway.* In 2007 he was invited to curate the theatre programme for the prestigious Kilkenny Arts Festival. He has worked as Director with Landmark Productions on productions of *Breaking Dad, Between Foxrock and a Hard Place,* and *The Last Days of the Celtic Tiger,* all by Paul Howard

PAULA MCCAFFERTY
SET DESIGNER

PAULA GRADUATED FROM Aberystwyth University with a degree in Scenography.

She has worked as a costume designer on several productions within Belfast; *Shoot The Crow* (Prime Cut Productions), *Still Life Still* (Prime Cut Productions), *Crimea Square* (Greenshoot Productions), *God of Carnage* (Prime Cut Productions). Paula has also worked as a production assistant for *First Love is the Revolution* in the Soho Theatre. This is her first professional stage design production.

SINEAD MCKENNA
LIGHTING DESIGNER

SINEAD HAS RECEIVED TWO Irish Times Theatre Awards for Best Lighting Design. Previous designs at Lyric Theatre include *Macbeth, Snow Queen* and *Merry Christmas Betty Ford*. Recent designs include *Grace Jones- Bloodlight and Bami* (Blinder Films); *Angela's Ashes The Musical*; *Futureproof* (Cork Everyman Palace); *Nivellis War* (Cahoots NI/ New Victory Theatre Broadway). Other designs include *The Becket/Pinter/Friel Festival, Private Lives (2016 and 2008), Juno and the Paycock, A month in the Country, The Gigli Concert, The Mariner, The Price and An Ideal Husband* (The Gate Theatre); *Maz and Bricks* (Fishamble), *The Wake, Othello, Aristocrats, Quietly, Alice in Funderland, The Plough and the Stars, 16 Possible Glimpses, The Burial at Thebes, Howie The Rookie, Finders Keepers* (Abbey Theatre); *New Electric Ballroom* (Druid); *Howie The Rookie, Greener, October, Last Days of The Celtic Tiger, Blackbird* (Landmark Productions); *Dubliners,* (The Corn Exchange), *Famished Castle, Travesties, The Importance of Being Earnest, Improbable Frequency* (Drama Desk nomination 2009 Best Lighting Design for a Musical), *The Parker Project, Life is a Dream, Attempts on her life and Dream of Autumn* (Rough Magic); *The Wolf and Peter, Agnes, Pageant, Swept* (Cois Ceim); *Invitation to a journey* (Coisceim/Fishamble/ Crash Ensemble); *Don Giovanni* (OTC); *La Traviata* (Malmo Opera House); *The Rape of Lucretia* IYO, *The Magic Flute, The Marriage of Figaro* (Opera Theatre Company), *Midsummer Night's Dream* (Opera Ireland). She has also worked with Decadent, Gar San Lazare, Corn Exchange, THISISPOPBABY, Siren, Second Age, Performance Corporation, Semper Fi and Guna Nua.

ÚNA HICKEY
COSTUME DESIGNER

ÚNA HICKEY IS A COSTUME DESIGNER from Belfast. She completed a Degree in Performance Costume at Edinburgh College of Art in 2006. Since then she has worked in costume for theatre, advertising, film, circus and dance both at home and abroad. Notable productions include Prime Cut's *I am my own wife* (Costume Designer), Opera NI's *Riders to the Sea* (Costume Designer), Prime Cut's *The Baths* (Costume Designer), HBO's *Game of Thrones* (Breakdown Artist, On Set Standby), Stuber Picture's *Your Highness* (Breakdown Artist) and Walden Media's *City of Ember* (Costume Assistant). Úna collaborates regularly with the Drama department at Queen's University Belfast, designing the costume for large productions and teaching aspiring designers.

CONOR MITCHELL
MUSIC DIRECTOR

CONOR MITCHELL IS A MUSIC-THEATRE MAKER from Northern Ireland. He is the recipient of the 2016 Arts Council Northern Ireland *Major Individual Artist's Award*. He is currently under commission for the Lyric Theatre. Recent scores include his music-theatre piece *The Habsburg Tragedies* (The Belfast Ensemble), his Cultural Olympiad opera *Our Day* (NI Opera), the children's opera *The Musician* (national tour), the choral work *Shadowtime* (Royal Festival Hall), *Requiem for the Disappeared* (Spark Opera), the sinfonietta *20: Ceasefire*, and his *Cabaret Songs* in celebration of Britten's 100th birthday (Aldeburgh Music). He and Mark Ravenhill's award winning song cycle *Ten Plagues* (Royal Court, Traverse Theatre) was recently revived at Wilton's Music Hall, London, performed again by Marc Almond. A reworking of his 2003 musical-theatre piece *Group!* has just premiered in Ireland, directed by the composer. As composer/librettist *The Incredible Book Eating Boy* (The MAC, Belfast), *The Dummy Tree* (National Theatre, London), *Geppetto In Spring* (Gothenburg,

Sweden), *Goblin Market, Christmas Betty Ford* (Lyric, Belfast), *Have A Nice Life* (Off Broadway), *The Last Ambulance* (The Gate, London) and many others including West End and off-Broadway. Awards include BEST SCORE (New York Musical Theatre Festival), the Stiles and Drewe Song Writers Award, The Arts Foundation Fellowship Award for Composition, awarded by Sir Richard Eyre and two Fringe Firsts. Mitchell is the founder of *The Belfast Ensemble*.

EMILY FORAN
ASSISTANT DIRECTOR

EMILY STUDIED THEATRE DIRECTING at The Lir Academy, Trinity College Dublin. Credits for the Lyric Theatre include *Pentecost* and *Locked In, Locked Out* as Assistant Director. Other Theatre credits as Director: *After the End* (The Lir Academy), *All The Way, Night Shift* and *Two Pricks in a Hotel Room* (Smock Alley Theatre), *Hey You!* (Accidental Theatre), *Fake I.D.* (Framework, Belfast Comedy Festival), *Pains of Youth* (Brian Friel Theatre). Credits as Assistant Director: *THESE ROOMS* (ANU Productions & Coisceim Dance Theatre), *Radamisto* (Northern Ireland Opera), *I Am a Camera* (The Lir Academy), *The Gentle Island* (Lughnasa International Friel Festival), *Catchpenny Twist* (Brian Friel Theatre). Emily will be directing the revival of her production of *After the End* in the Naughton Studio in February 2018 before transferring to the New Theatre Dublin.

Fire Below – a War of Words

Over the past twenty-five years Owen McCafferty's plays have been performed worldwide and have won numerous awards. Previous work includes *Titanic: Scenes from thr British Wreck Commissioner's Inquiry, 1912* (MAC, Belfast); *The Absence of Women* (Lyric Theatre, Belfast, and Tricycle Theatre, London); *Days of Wine and Roses* (Donmar Theatre, London; *Closing Time* (National Theatre, London); *Shoot the Crow* (Druid, Galway); *Mojo Mickybo* (Kabosh, Belfast); *Scenes from the Big Picture* (National Theatre, London), which won the Meyer-Whitworth, John Whiting and Evening Standard Awards; *Quietly* (Abbey Theatre, Dublin), which won the Writers' Guild Award for Best Play; and *Death of a Comedian* (Abbey Theatre, Dublin, Lyric Theatre, Belfast, and Soho Theatre, London). He is currently working on his first screenplay, *Normal People*, and a musical based on the novel *The Good Son*.

OWEN McCAFFERTY

Fire Below

a war of words

FABER & FABER

First published in 2017
by Faber and Faber Limited
74–77 Great Russell Street
London WC1B 3DA

Typeset by Country Setting, Kingsdown, Kent CT14 8ES
Printed and bound by CPI Group (UK) Ltd, Croydon, CRO 4YY

A CIP record for this book
is available from the British Library

ISBN 978-0-571-34526-7

2 4 6 8 10 9 7 5 3 1

Fire Below, a co-production between the Abbey Theatre, Dublin, and the Lyric Theatre, Belfast, was first performed on the Danske Bank stage of the Lyric Theatre, Belfast, on 12 October 2017, and subsequently on the Peacock stage of the Abbey Theatre, Dublin, on 7 November 2017. The cast, in order of appearance, was as follows:

Rosemary   Cara Kelly
Gerry   Frankie McCafferty
Tom   Ruairi Conaghan
Maggie   Ali White

Director   Jimmy Fay
Assistant Director   Emily Foran
Set Design   Paula McCafferty
Costume Design   Úna Hickey
Music and Sound Design   Conor Mitchell
Lighting Design   Sinead McKenna
AV Consultant   Neil O'Driscoll
Production Managers   Paul Hinchcliffe, Cliff Barragry
Casting Directors   Kelly Phelan, Clare Gault

Characters

Rosemary

Gerry

Tom

Maggie

all mid- to late fifties

FIRE BELOW

A WAR OF WORDS

Belfast. Hot summer evening.

They all drink wine whenever they want.
No one is at any time drunk.

No surtitles for anything spoken in Irish.

Rosemary and Gerry are sitting on their deck having a drink and looking out into the distance. Opera is playing in the background – it is barely audible.

Rosemary   do it

Gerry   no

Rosemary   it's liberating

Gerry   it's stupid

Rosemary lifts some coins from the table and throws them into the field adjacent to the house.

Rosemary   do it

Gerry   no

Rosemary   you're no fun – you can be funny – but you're no fun

Gerry   i'm not silly

Rosemary   no gerry you're not silly

Gerry   bonfire soon

Rosemary   now that's silly

Gerry   it's not something i'd ever do – burn stuff

Rosemary   but you'd watch others do it

Gerry   ditto

Rosemary   i'm only watching because you are

Gerry	sit on the deck – have a few drinks put the world to rights – and watch working-class protestants burn some tyres and sticks and shout some shit – if that can't make a middle-class ex-catholic happy what can
Rosemary	when we were kids we used to collect for the bonfire – we weren't allowed to watch it – but we collected for it – times have changed – no collecting now – but watching
Gerry	times have changed – does that bonfire offend you
Rosemary	i think it's stupid
Gerry	does it offend you though
Rosemary	gerry i'm fifty-seven years old – some eejits burn some old wood . . .
Gerry	what it represents – you know – we were brought up catholics – not that now – what it represents – does it offend you
Rosemary	if i thought about it i might be – times have changed – there's more important things in life than that – does it offend you
Gerry	don't know – in one sense no – not at all – has nothing to do with my life – other than i sit on the deck once a year – sometimes on my own sometimes with others – have a drink and look at the bonfire at the bottom of my garden – then – maybe – i don't know – maybe you need to think once in a while what the people round the bonfire think of you
Rosemary	do you really care

Gerry	don't know – lived in this house for twenty odd years – that estate's been at the bottom of our garden nearly all that time – never spoken to or met anyone from there – i'm not suggesting i wanted to i'm just saying i haven't – they might look up here and think who lives up there
Rosemary	no might about it – if you look down there they look up here
Gerry	do you care
Rosemary	i would care if i thought they hated me – i would care if i thought they were dancing round the bonfire thinking we were fenian bastards – i'd care then – if they're just doing what they do because they are who they are then no i don't care

Silence.

He pours wine for them both.

Gerry	where'd you get this
Rosemary	shipping direct – i got a case – they were doing a deal – you like it
Gerry	new zealand – i'm more chile
Rosemary	do you like it
Gerry	i'm not classy enough to dislike it
Rosemary	no
Gerry	new zealand seems too healthy a place for wine
Rosemary	nonsense

Gerry	it wasn't a serious comment – throw some more coins – be free
Rosemary	no
	Silence.
Gerry	did you phone the guy about the roof
Rosemary	i did – he says he can't do it because of the asbestos – but he gave the name of another builder – i left a message
Gerry	the ivy growing over that outhouse used to look beautiful now it's a pain in the arse – the roof bloody cave in under the weight of it
Rosemary	i've left a message
Gerry	it needs a new door and windows
Rosemary	i'll talk to him – get an estimate
Gerry	maybe we should just knock it down – have like a patio thing
Rosemary	it's too far from the house
Gerry	cut a path down to it
Rosemary	you say that now but you wouldn't use it – get a new roof on it – paint the walls white look like a cottage at the bottom of the garden – have flowers round it
Gerry	what's the point in having something that looks like a cottage but isn't a cottage – and no more flowers – i don't want anything else that grows – they have to be looked after – and i don't want any more of that – flame-thrower the whole lot then tarmac it – no looking after anything – maybe just one tree or something

Rosemary	you need a garden so you can potter around in it – give you something to do
Gerry	i've plenty to do – papers to mark – shit to make up
Rosemary	i mean in later life – keep yourself moving – what is it tom petty said – never slow down never grow old
Gerry	tom petty – in later life i'll either be dead or sitting on this deck with a glass of something looking out over the world – and now and again watching you potter around – that's if you're still here
Rosemary	i'll be here – if nothing else just out of spite
Gerry	good girl
	Silence.
Rosemary	when are they coming round
Gerry	don't know – about now – and by the way – don't you and tom be talking in irish half the night – it's ignorant – feels like you're whispering
Rosemary	nothing ignorant about it – whispering – good practice for him that's all
Gerry	aye – good practice for him
Rosemary	you should learn – join in
Gerry	no – if i was going to learn a language it wouldn't be irish – no use in the outside world – also too republican
Rosemary	it's not republican for tom

Gerry	he's a protestant – i get that – too republican for me – it would feel like a statement
Rosemary	statement – always good to have another language that's all
Gerry	spanish – i like the idea of speaking spanish – sounds emotional – irish sounds like you're about to hack up
Rosemary	take some spanish lessons then
Gerry	move to spain – live life on a balcony overlooking the beach – be good to look out on to something that wasn't belfast – although in saying that if you didn't know any better you wouldn't know this was belfast just by looking at it
Rosemary	except for the massive fire at the bottom of the garden
Gerry	except for the massive fire at the bottom of the garden

Tom and Maggie enter carrying bottles of wine.

	more wine we need more wine – we're new zealand this evening
Maggie	south africa
Gerry	travelling the world without leaving the deck

They sit.

Maggie	sorry we're late
Gerry	you're not late – nothing burning yet

Maggie	don't you just love the smell of napalm in the morning
Gerry	good line – great line
Tom	*cáide má 'tá tú*
Rosemary	*an mhaith go raibh mhaith agat – tá tú ag dul i bheabhas*
Tom	*go raibh maith agat – tá muinteoir maith agam*

Gerry and Maggie exchange a look.

Maggie	tom
Tom	practice – what is the distance between our two houses
Gerry	none – they're beside each other
Tom	door to door
Gerry	twenty yards
Tom	i consider myself to be a law-abiding citizen
Gerry	you are indeed a law-abiding citizen – a pillar of society – a rock
Tom	never a truer word spoken by a finer human – well . . .
Maggie	within twenty yards we've just had a row with one of those eastern european crowd that live off church road
Rosemary	i see them passing the house sometimes – nearly always drunk
Maggie	this one was drunk – people can live where ever they want – but they can't be drunk and look like they're going to have a piss outside your house

Gerry	i've seen tom drunk trying to have a piss outside your house – in a law-abiding way
Tom	that's different – you're allowed to piss outside your own house
Maggie	it is different – and no you're not allowed to do that – why do all men think it's alright to do that
Gerry	not all men
Rosemary	no woman would do it
Gerry	they would and they do
Rosemary	no they wouldn't and no they don't
Gerry	if you had to you would
Rosemary	that's different
Maggie	is it not reasonable to say to someone don't piss outside my house – he shouted at the two of us
Rosemary	did he understand what you were saying
Tom	yes i told him to fuck off – who doesn't understand fuck off
Rosemary	was he urinating
Maggie	he looked as if he might – he was fumbling around round his crotch
Gerry	is crotch still a word
Maggie	very funny
Gerry	you told some drunk foreign guy to fuck off and he shouted at you
Tom	correct

Maggie	he was going to take his dick out
Gerry	was he though
Tom	i didn't see – maggie said he's going to piss on our wall so i turned round and told him to fuck off
Gerry	protestants – what is it with you and foreigners
Tom	so because you're a catholic you'd let him piss on your wall
Gerry	i would enquire after his well being
Maggie	he was going to get his dick out
Tom	there's a crowd of them – all live in a house down there
Maggie	all men
Gerry	maybe they'll be down at the bonfire later
Tom	wouldn't think so – he was a catholic
Gerry	how do you know
Tom	smelt like one
Rosemary	*na seann chinn na cinn is fearr*
Tom	*is fearr*
Rosemary	best
Tom	best – *is fearr*
	Silence.
Gerry	we're thinking of knocking down the outhouse
Rosemary	we're not thinking of doing that

Gerry	thinking of it maybe
Rosemary	no – not thinking of it
Gerry	get a better view of the estate – if i ever want to throw anything at them i'll get a clear shot
Tom	better with a catapult
Gerry	a hand-held one – or one of those massive ones from the middle ages
Tom	you're always better with a massive one
Gerry	massive crotch
Rosemary	we're going to get rid of all the ivy and get a new roof – we just discovered that one's asbestos – got the name of a builder does that
Maggie	give me his number we're thinking of getting a bit of work done – might open up the back room on to the patio
Tom	we want to give the burglars a better view of our stuff – all those eastern european guys – let them see in so they know what life could be like – then make it easier for them to lift it all
Maggie	isn't the house alarmed – be lovely this time of year just to open it all up and walk out
Rosemary	we thought about that a few times – a lot of glass
Maggie	i like glass – i like the light
Gerry	yes light – if we had better weather i'd live out the back – that's the way we're meant to live – outside

Maggie	people in sunnier countries always seem to be happier
Tom	except the middle east
Gerry	must be a nightmare living there – too hot – sweltered
Tom	it's where they want to be
Maggie	the med and south america – spanish-type places
Gerry	i might learn spanish
Maggie	beautiful language – it sounds very passionate
Rosemary	*tá gaelige ró-dheachar dó*
Tom	*ró-deachar di comh maith*
Maggie	i'll take a class with you – i'd like to learn another language – other than irish – i don't see the point to that
Tom	*tá feidhm leis*
Gerry	like ulster scots – that's just country people speaking english – sucker upper and wee dafties – all that gibberish
Tom	easy to learn
Maggie	if we did spanish together gerry they could have their language and we could have ours – change the divide – spanish and irish instead of protestants and catholics
Gerry	we're not real protestants and catholics are we
Tom	not real ones no
Gerry	we're way beyond that – the people waiting to light that bonfire are real protestants

Maggie	and who are the real catholics
Rosemary	the ones hugging the altar rails – the blind faithers
Gerry	once you get educated there should be a natural drifting away from all that
Tom	we live in one of those black holes in space – slowly but surely dragging everything into the darkness
Maggie	it's politicians
Rosemary	it's always politicians – that estate was built about the same time as the good friday agreement – we sat here – it was a grubby wee patio then having a drink to celebrate it
Tom	the d'hondt system
Gerry	ofmdfm
Maggie	petitions of concern
Rosemary	it was a great night
Gerry	that's nearly twenty years ago
Tom	jesus
Rosemary	it felt like there was genuine hope in the air – everybody saying the same thing – a new beginning – *tús úr*
Tom	*tús úr*
Rosemary	we all sat on the patio drinking wine and looking down at the building site that was going to be the estate – it represented a new beginning – i never thought there'd be as many houses – more fields then – less people
Gerry	d'hondt – god bless d'hondt

Tom	cross-border institutions – every other word was cross-border institutions – never hear of them now – that can only mean one of two things – either they're gone or they're everywhere
Maggie	as long as they got rid of the shooting on the streets – that was the only thing that mattered – so that's the only thing they took care of
Tom	looking back – aye
Gerry	too much given to the working class – i don't mean that in a bad way – i just mean it needed a bit more balance
Rosemary	the middle class are always ignored when it comes to the decision end of things
Maggie	that's right – it's people who shout the loudest who get the most
Gerry	(*half shouts in the direction of the bonfire*) loudest – most
	Silence.
Tom	a patio down where the outhouse is
Rosemary	it's not being knocked down
Gerry	a patio would be lovely – sit away from the house – on my own – no woman's land
Tom	that's where you want to be – no woman's land
Rosemary	this is the way men decide things isn't it – they just keep repeating something until it happens or people think it's true – we're getting a new roof not knocking it down

Gerry	no woman's land – i could put a plaque up down there or something
Maggie	i wanted to call our house cherry hill – because of the cherry tree – and the hill
Rosemary	in irish that would be *cnoc na silin*
Tom	cherry hill – *cnoc na silin*
Maggie	it would've been in english
Gerry	what would it be in ulster scots – (*Rural accent.*) cherry hill
Rosemary	i know it would've been in english – cherry hill – lovely
Maggie	all the post would be addressed to cherry hill – if someone asked where you lived you'd say cherry hill
Tom	we live in belfast
Maggie	i just liked the name – he got on his high horse
Rosemary	*tá cosa fada a dhith ort le ghabhal ar capall ard*
Tom	i didn't get that
Rosemary	you need long legs for a high horse
	Silence.
	i don't know what i'd call this place if i was to give it a name
Gerry	we'd – what we'd call it
Tom	houses shouldn't have names – it's stupid
Gerry	ofmdfm
Rosemary	just call it the assembly

Gerry	i like that
Rosemary	*ard-oifig*
	Maggie stops Tom repeating Rosemary with a look.
Gerry	where do you live – the assembly
Tom	nice ring to it
Maggie	cherry hill – i'm going to pretend it's called that anyway
Gerry	the assembly on the hill – couldn't do any worse than the one we have
Tom	no – houses down in the estate would have good names i'd say
Gerry	orange grove
Maggie	very good
Gerry	orange parade
Tom	that would be a street
Maggie	i don't think that estate was meant to be like that
Tom	be like what – a kip
Rosemary	it's not a kip
Tom	it's a kip
Maggie	it wasn't meant to be just all the one side
Gerry	somebody must've decided something
Maggie	if it was being built at the time of the good friday agreement i don't see how they thought it was a good idea not to make it mixed

Tom	that's what's wrong with the working class – they don't like mixed areas – that's what's ruined this place – wasn't like that before
Rosemary	i agree with that – we were sitting on our patio looking at the building site – we were saying – how brilliant it would be to live overlooking a truly mixed estate – how that in itself promotes mixed education and eventually that spreads throughout society
Maggie	priests – there'll be no mixed education system while they're around – men
Gerry	nuns
Rosemary	nuns might as well be men
Maggie	priests didn't have anything to do with that estate – all it takes is for someone to say – i don't want to live beside that family – i don't want to do that – i don't want to do this – so instead of forcing people together – forcing people to live together – the politicians take the easy way out – right live with your own – there you go
Gerry	we should've protested – placards on the patio
Maggie	that's what's wrong – we don't protest enough – don't shout enough
Tom	what were we going to do – put a big banner across the back of the house – only people who think like us – we don't mind if they have slightly less money and drink cider instead of wine
Maggie	you know i'm right
Rosemary	you are right

Gerry	you are right
Tom	you are right – if right was a person it would be you
Maggie	oh piss off – hope they burn your outhouse to the ground
Gerry	so do i – could we build a house on that – a proper house
Tom	i enquired about that years ago – they won't give you planning permission
Maggie	something to do with living on the bend of a main road
Tom	access – easy access or safe access – something like that
Gerry	you enquired about building a house in my garden
Tom	yes – we were thinking of going back to the good old days when you could burn catholics out and take their houses – i was thinking about a house at the bottom of our garden
Gerry	so just a patio then
Maggie	protestants were burnt out as well
Rosemary	shut up
	A moment.
	we're just fixing the roof
	Silence.
Tom	the wine's nice
Rosemary	shipping direct
Maggie	i use them

Rosemary	there was a deal – fifty-seven pounds a case
Maggie	it's lovely – shipping direct are very knowledgeable – they really know what they're doing – i'm going to use them all the time now
Tom	we're on wine every night now
Maggie	just a glass or two
Tom	a bottle and a half
Rosemary	he'd drink that on his own
Gerry	you need a nightcap
Rosemary	you'd drink it out of a nightcap
Gerry	why is it women can drink what they want and it's fine but men are all pissheads
Maggie	because men are all pissheads
Rosemary	you see – everyone knows – it's a fact
Tom	this is the raw material we have to work with
Maggie	best thing ever happened to you – only for me you'd be more of a pisshead then you already are
Tom	i count my blessings dearest
Gerry	young love – there's nothing like it
Tom	go on say it – say it – and – this – is
Gerry	nothing like it

A cheer.

there's some activity down there – the matches are at the ready – the officials are in

	place and we're just waiting on the referee's whistle
Tom	something fascinating about fire
Gerry	false alarm – barbecue
Maggie	any word from maeve
Rosemary	she's in bolivia now
Maggie	i'd be worried sick
Rosemary	i am but what can you do
Gerry	i don't want the kids here – better off elsewhere – different life – where's your keith – leeds doing law – better off for it – what would he want to be back here for
Tom	exactly – say hello now and again on the phone – make sure they're alright – see if they need a few quid – no need to be hanging round here
Maggie	you miss them though
Rosemary	i talk to maive on skype
Maggie	it's brilliant
Gerry	another thing too – i don't want them to be made feel guilty for not coming back here and trying to make this a better place – i want them to make somewhere else a better place – or better still go to a place where they don't have to make it better because it's already good enough
Tom	if you're in belfast for a weekend it's meant to be good
Gerry	let them come home for a weekend then

Rosemary	i'd love to have gone away travelling
Gerry	we've been on holiday in spain or thereabouts every year for the last twenty years
Rosemary	i mean when i was young – on my own
Maggie	where would you have gone
Rosemary	don't know – a few places – vietnam – russia – nepal – i always liked the idea of cuba
Gerry	all poor places
Rosemary	for the experience of it
Gerry	aye – for the experience of it – couldn't see you in a tent in nepal somehow
Rosemary	not now – then – not now
Maggie	i've always wanted to go to israel
Gerry	israel
Maggie	for the history of it – see it for myself
Tom	any type of travelling is good – that's what's wrong with people here they don't travel enough – even if you're on a package holiday or something – take a walk down to the local shops
Gerry	is that why you speak irish
Tom	i'm making an effort
Gerry	you are tom – you're making an effort
Tom	*mhuin do bhean a lán dom*
Gerry	is that right – very good – i'll have to think about that and decide what action to take

Tom	what
Gerry	what – i've been taking irish classes – did rosemary not tell you
Rosemary	*níor inis – amadán*
	A tiny moment.
Gerry	got ya – had you worried there – cracked your wee code
Tom	no code to crack gerry – just speaking another language that's all
Gerry	what you say the last time – what was it
Tom	that i was making an effort and sometimes it was difficult
Maggie	they say the older you get the harder it is to learn a language
Gerry	fuck other languages – although in saying that i think if you live in another country it should be compulsory to learn the language of that country – there's nothing worse than foreigners speaking english that you can't understand – you have to keep saying i don't understand – they think you're being shitty with them – you can't say that though because it's racist – even though it's common sense
Tom	there's no common sense any more
Maggie	no common sense any more
Rosemary	people should always be respectful of where they live and abide by the rules of that country – if you don't want to do that you shouldn't go there

Tom	is that not common sense – but no – this is going to sound racist – but that doesn't mean it is racist – in some city in england – birmingham maybe – there was a big billboard advertising women's thongs
Rosemary	as you do
Gerry	you have to advertise them to sell them
Rosemary	thongs – i can tell you one thing for sure it wasn't a woman that invented them
Maggie	when they were in i liked them – they're not in now
Tom	can't remember you wearing them
Maggie	either you've a bad memory or you weren't there when i had them on
Rosemary	now you're talking
Tom	they were on the billboard – so there was a picture of four women – you couldn't see their faces – wearing different coloured thongs – and underneath it said thongs for the memories – so – it's meant to be funny – the billboard was beside a mosque – there were complaints made that it was offensive to those attending the mosque – both men and women – so it had to be taken down – it wasn't meant to be offensive it was just there to sell something – we are a western capitalist country – that's what we do and whoever lives here needs to understand that
Gerry	we don't live in england by the way
Tom	aye but it's the same – a few glasses of wine and he's all we don't live in england –

western capitalist country – it could happen
here just as easy – there's muslims popping
up everywhere

Maggie   that's true

Gerry   i see smoke

Tom   smoke

Gerry   this needs to be marked – we'll hum and
dance

Tom   hum to what

Gerry   if you leave me now by chicago

Tom   in the spirit of the good friday agreement
we'll swap partners

Gerry   girls

Maggie   right right

*Gerry starts humming the tune. They stand
up and move towards their dancing
partners – slowly dancing all the while.
They dance – it is a mixture of humming
and a few lines of the song. They are all out
of tune. They dance for as long as they
imagine the song lasts.*

Rosemary   will i change the music – get the dancing
going

Tom   yes

Maggie   later

Rosemary   it's not the right bonfire

Gerry   what way not right

Rosemary   i think that's just one for the kids

Tom	the kids
Rosemary	it's just a wee one – look – it must be a new thing
	They look.
Gerry	i was ready to go there – fuck that
	They sit. Silence.
Rosemary	it's brilliant sitting here and looking over the entire city – few people get a chance to do that
Maggie	i used to bring the kids out at night and make them stand there and look – i used to say to them – this is where you're from – this is your city
Rosemary	it's beautiful
Gerry	the lovely belfast
Tom	it's strange isn't it – those kids down there thinking setting fire to something is fun
Rosemary	all kids think setting fire to something is fun
Gerry	true – any bonfire – it doesn't matter what side or what it's pretending to celebrate – you shouldn't bring your kids like
Tom	that's right – you should always want something different for your kids – it's like the travel thing – you want them here but they're better off away
Maggie	you can't blame kids for standing round a bonfire
Gerry	it's a family thing – they're all down there

Maggie	if you were brought up like that you'd be down there
Gerry	that's the point – it's the way kids are brought up – it's the parents – it's always the parents
Rosemary	a friend of mine is a schoolteacher – different part of belfast – it's the same though – nightmare – she says parent-teacher meetings are a joke – she's sitting all dressed to the nines – the other side of the table two scrubbers in tracksuits – why's our jimmy – or whatever – not doing well at school – she has to pretend that everyone's trying – and wee jimmy this and wee jimmy that – the real truth is they sit in the house all day smoking joints – and then she puts toothpaste on his dick – because apparently everyone is doing these days – what chance has wee jimmy got
Tom	toothpaste on the dick is it
Gerry	how bored do you need to get – what's going on in your head to think – you know that stuff we use to clean our teeth – what about you put some on my dick and then we'll have a ride and see how that goes
Maggie	i thought it was for blowjobs
Gerry	right – hadn't thought of that
Maggie	why would you
Rosemary	no i think it's for intercourse
Gerry	intercourse – intercourse – what's that
Tom	intercourse – never heard of it

Rosemary	*suirí – ag deanamh suirí*
Gerry	toothpaste – have to give that a burl
Rosemary	it's difficult enough to get you to put it on your teeth
Tom	teeth – toothpaste – that's the old way – the working class – all that shit – it is my right to put toothpaste on my dick – and if i want my child to spend his time dicking up the toothpaste that's his right
Gerry	would anyone like to partake in a massive spliff of skunk
Maggie	a massive spliff of skunk
Gerry	that's what they're at during the day – all they do is sit around and smoke blow
Tom	that sounds like a good way to spend your day actually
Gerry	that's tomorrow sorted then
Tom	we could go on the march – go to the field – make a picnic of it
Gerry	march march march march march
Rosemary	my dad's friend – a catholic – used to go to the field
Maggie	you could do things like that years ago
Rosemary	he worked in the fruit market – sold flowers at it – why would people be buying flowers at the field
Tom	don't know – never been – flowers doesn't seem right
Gerry	orange lilies

Tom	orange lilies
Rosemary	made a fortune
Gerry	we're sitting here watching this and these pictures go out all over the world
Rosemary	pictures of us – should've done my hair
Maggie	imagine people were watching us doing this – if they didn't hear what we were saying they wouldn't know what we were doing
Gerry	stupid – idiotic – pictures of people burning stuff – they go out all over the world – that's who the rest of the world think we are – bloody third-world image
Maggie	we need the spotlight – all got too used to it
Rosemary	that's the problem isn't it – once the spotlight is on you it's difficult to move away from it – politicians here still think we're on the world stage
Gerry	the one i hate is politicians from here going to the white house for saint patrick's day – nonsense – i don't care about saint patrick's day right – but – if you're going to celebrate saint patrick's day you'd think you'd celebrate it in his country – but no – have to go to america to celebrate it – you know what that's all about
Maggie	saying you've been to the white house
Gerry	correct – it's also a working-class thing – it's about getting to the white house – come from nothing now i'm in the white house – as if a black president cared about saint patrick's day

Maggie	that's right
Rosemary	not high on his agenda
Tom	irish vote in america – right – what do those shit-kickers eat and drink – bog water and turf
Rosemary	before i did my law degree i went to america for a month – do you have tv in ireland – do you have fish in ireland – jesus christ – a civil war – this guy actually said to me – civil war – that must be great – and now we run over there because they dye the rivers green – useless bloody place
Gerry	america – always makes me think that we can't look after our own affairs
Maggie	we can't
Tom	if it was solely left to business it would be sorted out – business people – like the mafia – know all this world terrorism stuff – get the mafia to sort that out – over and done within days
Gerry	just sitting here talking and drinking things are sorted out within seconds – just like that – a click of the fingers – mafia – terrorism – over – education and alcohol – there isn't a problem in the world that can't be sorted out with those two things – terrorism – mafia – done – sorted
Maggie	it's a serious thing though
Gerry	what is
Maggie	terrorism
Tom	that's why the mob are the boys to sort it out

Maggie	innocent people die – it's not a joke
Tom	what are you doing – we're not – it's just talk
Maggie	i'm just saying
Tom	is that right – were you in the middle of it all
Maggie	because you're not in the middle of something doesn't mean you can't have an opinion about it – or it doesn't affect you
Gerry	narrative – isn't that the in word at the moment – narrative – any type of debate about anything – any moment in history – anything – what you have to do is control the narrative
Rosemary	*srian ar an scéal*
Gerry	what
Rosemary	control the narrative
Tom	it's right though
Maggie	it is right yes – i have a narrative tom – i have a story to be listened to
Rosemary	we all do – but the working class has the narrative here – i know it's treated like a crime to say that – but that doesn't make it any less true
Tom	narrative – narrative – narrative – we all have a narrative
Rosemary	*nach dóigh libh go bhfuil smacht againn*
Tom	yes – didn't i just say so
Rosemary	*sin an déil*

Tom	*aontaím*
Rosemary	good boy
Gerry	good boy
Rosemary	the narrative that we come from . . .
Tom	middle class
Rosemary	for want of a better phrase – yes
Maggie	why for want of a better phrase
Rosemary	i don't know – you're right – middle class
Maggie	that's the problem – it's as if who we are has become a thing of shame – here we are sitting on a deck drinking wine together – the protestant and catholic middle classes – that's a brilliant thing – something to be proud of – not down at that bonfire but up here being civilised
Gerry	civilised
Tom	once that wine's finished and we drink more – civilised – don't think that's the word
Maggie	that's true – rosemary and i are civilised – yous two are just – not sure what the term is
Rosemary	they already know – drunken shitheads
Maggie	drunken shitheads
Gerry	i hate the way yous do that – as if it's a male thing
Rosemary	we've already explained – it is a male thing
Gerry	so you – really – don't drink as much as me
Rosemary	no

Gerry	you sure about that
Rosemary	i handle it better than you do
Tom	you two are just as bad
Gerry	handle it better
Rosemary	yes handle it better – don't make an eejit out of myself
Gerry	what is this – it's us you're talking to here – so you don't drink two bottles of wine get up on the deck and dance – to no music – like a complete balloon
Rosemary	i didn't earlier
Gerry	hadn't reached the two-bottle mark then
Rosemary	i carry the music in my head by the way
Maggie	yes you do
Rosemary	the wine is because we're repressed – depressed – compressed – isn't that right maggie
Maggie	yes all of that – you couldn't drink enough wine to kill the shit that we women have to carry around with us
Tom	you carry nothing around
Maggie	carry it around – oh yes – big backpack full of shit
Tom	give over
Rosemary	i refuse to admit i dance like a balloon
Maggie	you do dance like a bit of a mad woman
Rosemary	jumped ship there very quick

Maggie	say what you see – roy walker – catchphrase
Tom	close but it's not the one
Gerry	roy walker – the man's a star – you know that nonsense they had up in derry – city of culture guff – we're the city of culture
Tom	city of culture – jesus – londonderry
Gerry	they had this big comedy night in derry – roy walker was the main act – i was told he stole the show – in derry – so this is the joke he opened with – very droll – i used to go out with a girl from derry – lovely girl – she worked in the shirt factory – it was my birthday and for my present she got me a new shirt – after i tried it on i said to her – is there any chance this shirt is a second – she said yes how did you know – i said because one of the arms is longer than the other two – the place erupted – the man's a genius
Rosemary	never mind him – i don't dance like a balloon
Tom	you dancing *lámha agus cosa*
Rosemary	no no no
Gerry	don't say anything – don't say anything – this is how you know it's true – i bet you he said something like – arms and legs everywhere
Rosemary	he didn't smart arse – he said you dance with grace and elegance
Gerry	if grace and elegance is all arms and legs then yes i agree – tom
Tom	all arms and legs

Gerry	maggie show her – you do her the best
Rosemary	do her the best
Maggie	we had a competition – the surrounding community was invited – i was voted the one that did you the best
Rosemary	what a bitch
Maggie	i'm doing this for your own good – the cure sometimes needs to be painful
	Maggie stands and does a dance that is all arms and legs. She sits to applause.
Gerry	encore encore
Tom	bravo bravo
Rosemary	all so damn smart – that's nothing like it – not even close – what i do is interpret the music – i let the music take over my body and soul – i become the music – i am the music
Gerry	you are the music
Rosemary	fuck you – watch and learn
	Rosemary moves to the middle of the deck. She dances in much the same way Maggie did but just slightly 'better'. Tom joins her. He hums and sings a few words of 'The Sash'. Maggie joins them. They dance until the moment after it has stopped being fun and is just slightly embarrassing. They sit down.
Rosemary	can't dance my arse
Gerry	a star is born
Rosemary	better than those eejits round that fire

Tom	that's what i love about this – the ability just to get on with it – not ignore things but just get on with it – what were we talking about earlier on
Maggie	roy walker
Gerry	the man's a genius – say what you see
Tom	close but it's not the one
Gerry	say what you see – i might make that our family motto
Tom	or we could name our house that
Maggie	it's too long
Tom	say what you see
Maggie	he's not that funny
Tom	no idea – you've no idea – narrative and the middle class being forgotten in all this – and then we just slip into some other stuff – it doesn't linger – it's just there to be talked about – i love that – that's who we are – that's what the middle class is
Maggie	my mum was a doctor in a and e – not many women – not many catholics – but that could've been sorted out – civil rights could've done that – didn't need the ira for that to happen
Tom	no
Gerry	from roy walker to the civil rights – the middle class way
Rosemary	i agree
Tom	certainly – no need for all those killings

Maggie	murders
Tom	murders
Gerry	murders – killings – all still dead
Tom	that's true
Maggie	can you imagine what she saw – shootings – bombs – all those people in bits – day after day people being brought in in bits – you can't just keep looking at that and it not mean something – she was driving home after her shift this day – late in the afternoon – whenever she tells this she always says how beautiful a day it was – during the summer of nineteen seventy-four – driving home tired after a hard shift – she heard an explosion and saw that it was up ahead of her – she pulled the car over and run up to see if she could help out – a bomb had gone off in a bar – she said it was carnage – everything inside outside and bits of people everywhere – she found out later that six men had been blown up in that bar while they were watching a world cup football match on the tv – she always remembered that one incident – not because it was any different from any other explosion – but because there was nothing she could do – all those six men were already dead – blown to pieces – she was just standing there looking – she said it made her feel hopeless – to be honest i don't think it was something that ever really left her – and now because she lives in a nice house and has enough money to do her so she doesn't want for anything she's forgotten about

Tom   when i was at university studying law i used to always think this but never had the courage to say it – it has to do with the word hijacked – remember when we were kids the word hijacked was always being said on the news – not just the local news the world news as well – it was always a plane has been hijacked and taken to egypt – and here it was a bus has been hijacked and burnt

Gerry   still burning stuff now

Tom   i always thought my life – or part of it anyway – had been hijacked – nothing ever happened to me directly but we were all affected – by a so-called war that was happening in some places but not others – it was never really on my doorstep – but that doesn't mean in some way it didn't take its toll – if it hadn't have happened how do you know what type of people we might've been – held to ransom – not involved but held to ransom – the feeling i'm talking about has to do with not moving on in life or something – you know the reason i started to learn irish

Rosemary   *múinteoir maith faighte agat*

Gerry   english – english

Rosemary   the good friday agreement – you told me that

Tom   that's right – it's not a big deal – it doesn't mean much in the whole scheme of things – but to me it felt like progression that a protestant learns to speak irish

Gerry	i brought the kids to see ulster in the rugby – same type of thinking – it doesn't mean you have to go all the time – it's just enough that an effort was made – people don't make an effort here – if i'm going to make one why shouldn't they
Maggie	precisely – i agree with tom – i think the majority here were held to ransom by the few
Tom	and it's still happening
Rosemary	and it's still happening – see all the money spent on parades and that – how you stop all that nonsense is just let them go ahead – but no police protection – let them all beat the crap out of each other – who cares – they'll soon stop when they get tired
Tom	i agree – it's ridiculous – northern ireland could've worked in some way – and i'm not saying it's not working now – worked better – if the whole place hadn't been – and it still is – held to ransom by the working classes – and that's right across the board – both catholics and protestants
Maggie	it's to do with education
Gerry	education education education – without it nothing can be discussed properly
Tom	we discuss things properly – you think it was a crime to say you were educated – and that others should be
Gerry	nothing's ever solved
Rosemary	that suits people here – if you truly wanted to solve something here it would require

genuine change – and people here don't
want change

Gerry   this is the truth of the matter – those people
            standing round that – as yet to be lit –
            bonfire are standing there because they are
            stupid – they know no better – they were
            told something when they were kids and
            they have believed it ever since – and they
            tell their kids the same shit and so on and so
            on – that's it – that's all that happens here –
            the stupid run the place – not regarding
            money – because nobody's that stupid that
            they'd let the stupid look after the money –
            but they've been allowed to halt progress
            because they're listened to too much – and
            i don't mean any of that in a bad way

Tom   of course not – that's what's wrong isn't it –
            common sense – no one wants to deal with
            common sense any more

Maggie   correct – it's about being able to discuss
            things – discuss them in a rational way –
            whenever there's a problem at work – one
            of the junior accountants has dropped the
            ball – which happens a lot – most of them
            are useless – all just in it for the money – no
            respect for the job – for the profession – not
            brought up to respect anything – when the
            ball is dropped i think about how to solve the
            problem in a rational way – no histrionics –
            just an attempt to solve the situation – i
            think – personally – that has to do with
            being properly educated – and having
            respect – we were brought up to have
            respect – for others – for institutions – all
            of that

Gerry	it's about being detached – looking at something from a distance – only then do you have a good idea what it's about – then you can make an attempt to solve it – the reason those people down there – and i'm not making any comment or judgement about them – the reason they can't see the bonfire for what it is is because they're too close to it – not detached – no distance – we're detached – we can see from a distance
Tom	yet we've to listen to them – the only picture the rest of the world sees is their picture
Gerry	correct – we're the ones that are trapped – not them – us – trapped and not listened to
Maggie	trapped and not listened to
Rosemary	we need freedom people – we need liberation
	She takes some coins and throws them over the hedge.
	do it
Tom	why
Rosemary	did i just not say – freedom and liberation
Gerry	there is no reason why – it's stupid
	Maggie throws her coins.
Maggie	very good i like that
Rosemary	see – simple but brilliant
	Tom throws his coins.
Tom	i think i get it but it feels like a bit of a waste as well

Gerry	correct – someone could be doing with that
Rosemary	think bigger
Gerry	i think big alright – i just don't throw money away
Rosemary	the point is – that's not money – that's not even the point – it's a bit of fun – it doesn't matter
Maggie	do you think if it were pound coins it would be more exciting
Tom	no
Rosemary	don't think about it too much – it's just something stupid to do
Gerry	talking of things stupid i see movement down there – starting to put flags on the bonfire – that means they're getting ready to light it
Tom	is that a designated bonfire then
Gerry	must be – look at that
Tom	what
Gerry	they're getting a child – a wee lad – to climb up the bonfire and put the flags on it – jesus christ – is that not we've been talking about all night – what chance has that wee lad got if his parents think it's a great thing that he's the one picked to climb up the bonfire and put flags on it – and this all takes place in a playground – that says it all like
Tom	didn't one of the bonfires somewhere get it wrong and burn the flag of nigeria – thought it was a tricolour – eejits

Gerry	oh aye – all of that – i love the idea that they adopt flags from other parts of the world that they think connected to their cause – don't even know where the friggin places – like protestants and israel
Tom	and catholics and gaza and the west bank and that
Gerry	they burn the palestinian flag down there
Tom	ah well

Silence.

Rosemary	will i go in and get some cava or will the wine do us
Gerry	the wine'll do

Silence.

Maggie	they should ban burning tyres – not good for the environment – and if there's a wind we get all that over our houses
Gerry	you're right you don't want that
Rosemary	it should be more eco-friendly
Tom	what way
Rosemary	burn stuff from your garden
Tom	what happens if you're not near gardens
Rosemary	we can all drop off our garden waste in our range rovers to the wee working-class places
Tom	don't think they'd be happy about that
Rosemary	*bhí mé ag magadh*
Tom	were you

Rosemary	irish
Tom	too much wine – can't get my head round it – can understand it but can't work out how to say it now
Rosemary	right – and yes i was – joking
Gerry	what does – ah well – mean
Tom	it means – ah well – there you go
Gerry	there you go what
Tom	the stupid people are burning some foreign flag – there you go – they're entitled to do it aren't they – free expression and that
Gerry	what flag are we talking about here tom
Tom	the palestinian one
Gerry	you think they should burn the palestinian flag
Tom	i don't think they should burn any flags
Gerry	but
Tom	but i don't really have a problem with them burning that one – in terms of it being a genuine protest
	Silence.
Rosemary	protest about what
Maggie	let's just watch the fire
Rosemary	protest about what
Tom	about actions taken in other parts of the world – even the stupid are allowed opinions about world events

Gerry	they wouldn't know the fuck where palestine is
Tom	maybe not – but i do
Gerry	do you agree with israel
Tom	yes
Maggie	so do i – i assume we're allowed to
Rosemary	of course you're allowed to
Gerry	what say we just sit and wait for the bonfire to go up
Tom	prepare ourselves for the mighty blaze
	Silence.
Maggie	i read that hamas are attempting to negotiate a new arms deal with north korea – now no matter what you think that can't be good
Rosemary	but it's alright for israel to be armed to the teeth
Maggie	israel has to defend itself – what other way is there to do it but to be armed
Gerry	armed – fuckin armed – they've enough weapons to blow everyone to kingdom come
Maggie	good
Rosemary	so you see nothing wrong with that
Maggie	no – in fact they should be sold more
Rosemary	sold more – sold fuckin more
Maggie	yes sold fuckin more – the arab world would destroy that country if they could

53

Gerry	nonsense
Tom	that's not nonsense – they would and we all know it
Gerry	even if that were true – and it isn't
Maggie	it is
Gerry	even if it were true that doesn't give them the right to oppress another people – since nineteen forty-five the palestinians have been refugees in their own land
Maggie	if it were here what would you do
Rosemary	it was here
Maggie	not on the same scale
Rosemary	it's the same thing
Maggie	if rockets were being fired into this country day and daily – what would you do – how would you react
Tom	the last time – the last dispute
Gerry	dispute – fuckin dispute – they deliberately target civilian areas you know that
Maggie	hamas – yes i know
Gerry	very good
Tom	the last conflict – what did netanyahu say
Gerry	i don't give a fuck what that bastard says
Tom	he compared what's happening to israel to what happened to london and the blitz
Gerry	jesus christ – and you're ok with that
Tom	i get where he's coming from because it raises the question – what do you do

Rosemary	i'll tell you what you do – you stop oppressing the people who are firing the rockets – because that's the reason they're firing them – they killed nearly a thousand palestinians – about forty israelis were killed – over twenty per cent of that thousand were children – they fucking know they're killing children
Tom	the situation is about security – israel is being attacked so it has to defend itself – if that wasn't the situation life would be far better in gaza and on the west bank – they are only doing what any country would do
Gerry	it's the equivalent of mick tyson repeatedly punching a baby that's spitting at him – and the baby can't move to escape the blows – because there's hundreds of other babies crowded into the same room – and you know what – they'd fuckin blow that room up too and it wouldn't bother them
Tom	do you hear yourself when you say things like that – the state has a duty to protect its citizens against terrorism
Rosemary	what about state terrorism
Maggie	i'm sick to bloody death at that – any state that defends itself is also committing acts of terrorism – terrorists are bloody terrorists – that's it – end of story
Rosemary	so that's it – the palestinians are terrorists – and israel can do what it likes
Maggie	i didn't say they could do what they like – i said they have the right to defend themselves in whatever way they see fit

Rosemary	so they do what they like
Maggie	that's it isn't it – no one cares what's already there – generations of people living their lives out somewhere – providing the country with wealth – making it strong and secure – fighting for their country – giving their lives for something noble – but none of that matters – let's just speak up for the terrorists – the bombers – the murders
Gerry	sderot cinema – you ever hear of that – a group of israelis sat in lawn chairs – lawn chairs – like the ones we're sitting in – eating popcorn and watching all the missiles raining down on gaza – what's noble about that
Tom	you think they don't cheer in gaza when they trail a dead israeli soldier through the streets – it is what it is
Gerry	it is what it is – fuck
	Silence.
Maggie	i'm going home
Rosemary	yeah – you should
Maggie	i was going to say i can't believe you think like that but it doesn't really surprise me
Rosemary	why because we're catholics
Maggie	yes
Gerry	go on fuck off the both of yous
Tom	scrubbers – always have been always will be
Gerry	go on and fuck off – take your cheap wine down to the bonfire – it's where the two of yous belong

Tom	why don't you two fuck off down to dublin – that's where you really want to be – leave this country to us – we built it – it's ours
Gerry	fuck off to finchley you dickhead
Tom	nowhere – going nowhere – do you hear that – this is our country – we're going nowhere – our country – our fucking country

Tom and Maggie leave.

Rosemary	*chur mé m'am amú leatsa – an chaint sin uilig – an machnamh sin uilig – caite – curtha amú ortsa – tháinig tusa chugamsa – cuimhní ar sin. cuimhní i gconaí ar sin – tháinig tusa chugamsa a phleidhce bhradaigh – dál an scéil – níl a dheath 'mhaith ionat cibé – an taon fáth gur inis mé sin duit nó gur duine deas mé agus níor tógadh mé le fuath a bheith agam ar dhaoine eile – a ghadaí gan náire – you shit bag.*

They sit and pour a glass of wine.

Gerry	what was all that about
Rosemary	nothing
Gerry	it was about something
Rosemary	i was giving out to him – i wanted him to hear it in irish – wanted to annoy her
Gerry	right

Silence.

Rosemary	i'm not sitting here watching that shit
Gerry	nah – fuck it

They take the wine and exit.

The bonfire is lit – a red glow.

Gerry enters. He sits at the table and drinks his glass of wine.

my land – my garden – my deck – i'll do what i want – watch what i want – drinking my wine minding my own business – everyone should drink wine on their deck and mind their own business – look at whatever you want – the city – the sky

Rosemary enters.

Rosemary	thought you had enough of this
Gerry	taking a different approach – going to look up at the sky

Rosemary sits.

or across at the city – up or across – not down

Rosemary	the city looks beautiful from here
Gerry	it does – all those lights – all those houses – who the fuck lives there – no different from looking up in the sky – know as much about those stars as I do about the people in those houses
Rosemary	you've had too much wine
Gerry	aye – the world's allowed to be beautiful you know
Rosemary	i just said the city looks beautiful from up here
Gerry	so you did – so you did – you look beautiful
Rosemary	gerry

Gerry	what
Rosemary	nothing
Gerry	you do
Rosemary	thank you – just sit back there and look up at the sky
Gerry	sometimes when i'm sitting here on my own at night – there's a complete silence about the place – all around – everywhere

Tom and Maggie enter. They stand for a moment before sitting.

A lengthy silence.

They drink wine.

Tom	as if you'd know where finchley is
Gerry	do you know where it is
Tom	in england
Gerry	very good
Maggie	london
Rosemary	north-west london
Gerry	i knew that
Maggie	no you didn't
Rosemary	yous two know nothing
Tom	know enough

Lights begin to fade.

Gerry	correct know enough – did your man come back and piss on the wall
Tom	didn't look

Maggie	why would he come back to piss on the wall – although i wouldn't put it past them – but why would he
Gerry	i was only asking – i'm going to learn spanish – that's it – going to do it
Rosemary	good man
Tom	that fire doesn't last long
Rosemary	only a wee one not worth the waiting on
Gerry	spanish
Maggie	we know
Gerry	right – spanish

A slight red glow.

Blackout.

Appendix

TRANSLATIONS

PAGE 17

Tom *Cáide má 'tá tú*

how have you been keeping

Rosemary *an mhaith go raibh maith agat – tá tú gabháil i bfheabhas*

very well thank you – you're getting better at this

Tom *go raibh maith agat – tá múinteoir maith agam*

thank you – have a good teacher

PAGE 19

Rosemary *na sean chinn na cinn is fearr*

the old ones are the best

Tom *is fearr*

best

Tom best – *is fearr*

best –

PAGE 21

Rosemary *tá Gaelige ró-dheachar dó*

irish is too difficult for him

Tom *ró-dheachar di chomh maith*

too difficult for her as well

Tom *tá feidhm leis*

there's a point to it

Rosemary   it felt like there was genuine hope in the air – everybody saying the same thing – a new beginning – *tús nua*

a new beginning

Tom   *tús nua*

a new beginning

Rosemary   in irish that would be – *cnoc silíní*

cherry hill

Rosemary   *tá cosa fada a dhith ort le ghabhail ar capall ard*

you need long legs for a high horse

Rosemary   *ard-oifig*

headquarters

Tom   *mhuin do bhean a lán dom*

your wife has taught me a lot

Rosemary   *níor inis – amadán*

no he hasn't – eejit

Rosemary   *suirí – ag deanamh suirí*

intercourse – sexual intercourse – full penetrative sexual intercourse

PAGE 39

Rosemary *srian ar an scéal*
 control the narrative

PAGE 40

Rosemary *nach dóigh libh go bhfhuil smacht againn*
 do you not think we do

Rosemary *sin an déil*
 that's the deal

Tom *aontaim*
 I do

PAGE 42

Tom *lámha agus cosa*
 all arms and legs

PAGE 46

Rosemary *múinteoir maith faighte agate*
 you found a good teacher

PAGE 52

Rosemary *mé ag magadh*
 I was joking

PAGE 57

Rosemary *chur mé m'am amú leatsa – an chaint sin uilig –*
 an machnamh sin uilig – caite – curtha amú
 ortsa – thánig tusa chugamsa – cuimhní ar sin.
 cuimhní i gConaí ar sin – tháinig tusa chugamsa

a phleidhce bhradaigh – dál an scéil, níl a dheath
'mhaith ionat cibé – an taon fáth gur inis mé sin
duit nó gur duine deas mé agus níor tógadh mé
le fuath a bheith agam ar dhaoine eile – a ghadaí
gan náire – you shit bag.

wasted my bloody time with you – all that talk –
all that thinking – wasted – wasted on you – you
came to me – remember that – always remember
that – you came to me – you bastard – and by
the way you're shit at it – only tell you you're
good because i'm a nice person and i wasn't
brought up to hate people the way you were you
shit bag